Excel 2024 Conditional Formatting

EASY EXCEL 2024 ESSENTIALS - BOOK 2

M.L. HUMPHREY

CONTENTS

Introduction

This book is part of the *Easy Excel 2024 Essentials* series of titles. These are targeted titles that are excerpted from the main *Excel 2024 Essentials* series and are focused on one specific topic.

If you want a more general introduction to Excel, then you should check out the *Excel 2024 Essentials* titles instead; in this case, *Intermediate Excel 2024* which covers conditional formatting as well as a number of other topics, including pivot tables and charts.

But if all you want is a book that covers this specific topic, then let's continue with a discussion of how to apply conditional formatting to a range of cells based upon their contents.

Two-Variable Analysis Grid

Before we move on to our next tool in Excel, conditional formatting, I want to real quickly show you how to build what I call a two-variable analysis grid.

This is a table of values that represent the outcome of combining two different variables. For example, hours worked and pay. The higher your pay, the less you need to work to make the same amount, right? Or you can make up for earning less per hour by working more hours.

A two-variable analysis grid puts that information into a very practical lookup table which is simple to build, and which I'm going to use in the next chapter.

Okay. First thing you need to do is build the table with the values you want to use:

	A	B	C	D	E	F	G	H	I
1			Hours Worked						
2			20	25	30	35	40	45	50
3	Pay Rate	$15							
4		$20							
5		$25							
6		$30							
7		$35							
8		$40							
9		$45							
10		$50							

Building this involved a lot of the basic formatting we already covered in *Excel 2024 for Beginners*. I merged and centered the header sections across the cells, added fill color, changed the font color, centered the values I wanted to use, changed the text orientation along the left-hand side, and added borders:

Now we need to figure out the formula. In this case it's pretty basic, because we want to multiply hours times pay. In Cell C3 that would be:

=B3*C2

so I typed that in there.

Now, here's the fun part. We don't have to rewrite that formula for every cell in the table. Instead, we can change the formula so that it continues to reference Row 2 and Column B, but adjusts otherwise. Then we can just copy it.

You do that by putting a dollar sign in front of the part of each cell reference that you want to keep the same. Like so:

$$=\$B3*C\$2$$

I put a dollar sign in front of the B in B3 and in front of the 2 in C2. Now when I copy that formula to all of the other cells in the table, the formula in each cell will continue to reference Column B and Row 2 but will otherwise adjust. Like this:

	A	B	C	D	E	F	G	H	I
1						Hours Worked			
2			20	=C2+5	=D2+5	=E2+5	=F2+5	=G2+5	=H2+5
3		15	=$B3*C$2	=$B3*D$2	=$B3*E$2	=$B3*F$2	=$B3*G$2	=$B3*H$2	=$B3*I$2
4	Pay Rate	=B3+5	=$B4*C$2	=$B4*D$2	=$B4*E$2	=$B4*F$2	=$B4*G$2	=$B4*H$2	=$B4*I$2
5		=B4+5	=$B5*C$2	=$B5*D$2	=$B5*E$2	=$B5*F$2	=$B5*G$2	=$B5*H$2	=$B5*I$2
6		=B5+5	=$B6*C$2	=$B6*D$2	=$B6*E$2	=$B6*F$2	=$B6*G$2	=$B6*H$2	=$B6*I$2
7		=B6+5	=$B7*C$2	=$B7*D$2	=$B7*E$2	=$B7*F$2	=$B7*G$2	=$B7*H$2	=$B7*I$2
8		=B7+5	=$B8*C$2	=$B8*D$2	=$B8*E$2	=$B8*F$2	=$B8*G$2	=$B8*H$2	=$B8*I$2
9		=B8+5	=$B9*C$2	=$B9*D$2	=$B9*E$2	=$B9*F$2	=$B9*G$2	=$B9*H$2	=$B9*I$2
10		=B9+5	=$B10*C$2	=$B10*D$2	=$B10*E$2	=$B10*F$2	=$B10*G$2	=$B10*H$2	=$B10*I$2

The formula in Cell I10 is

$$=\$B10*I\$2$$

Pretty cool, huh?

(You can see all the formulas in a worksheet by going to the Formulas tab and clicking on Show Formulas under Formula Auditing. That's why you can also see that I built the values used in the table with formulas. I told you, I'm lazy.)

Here are the actual results of the calculations:

C3			fx	=$B3*C$2				
	A	B	C	D	E	F	G	H	I
1					Hours Worked				
2			20	25	30	35	40	45	50
3		$15	$300	$375	$450	$525	$600	$675	$750
4		$20	$400	$500	$600	$700	$800	$900	$1,000
5	Pay Rate	$25	$500	$625	$750	$875	$1,000	$1,125	$1,250
6		$30	$600	$750	$900	$1,050	$1,200	$1,350	$1,500
7		$35	$700	$875	$1,050	$1,225	$1,400	$1,575	$1,750
8		$40	$800	$1,000	$1,200	$1,400	$1,600	$1,800	$2,000
9		$45	$900	$1,125	$1,350	$1,575	$1,800	$2,025	$2,250
10		$50	$1,000	$1,250	$1,500	$1,750	$2,000	$2,250	$2,500

Do the math yourself, and you'll see that it worked for each of the cells.

Okay, now let's go use this table to demonstrate conditional formatting.

Conditional Formatting

Conditional formatting is a great way to visualize differences in your data. You can think of it as having Excel go through your results and highlight or otherwise call out results that meet various criteria. Just this week I used it to identify some duplicates in a list of values I had, but more often I use it to identify the "best" or "worst" in a range or to show how a range of values compare to one another.

Let's dive in and look at some examples because this one is very visual.

Looking at the analysis grid we built in the last chapter, let's say we know that you need to earn at least $1,200 a week. We can use conditional formatting to analyze the results in that table and color code them so that all values over $1199 are shaded in green.

Here that is:

	A	B	C	D	E	F	G	H	I
1					Hours Worked				
2			20	25	30	35	40	45	50
3		$15	$300	$375	$450	$525	$600	$675	$750
4	Pay Rate	$20	$400	$500	$600	$700	$800	$900	$1,000
5		$25	$500	$625	$750	$875	$1,000	$1,125	$1,250
6		$30	$600	$750	$900	$1,050	$1,200	$1,350	$1,500
7		$35	$700	$875	$1,050	$1,225	$1,400	$1,575	$1,750
8		$40	$800	$1,000	$1,200	$1,400	$1,600	$1,800	$2,000
9		$45	$900	$1,125	$1,350	$1,575	$1,800	$2,025	$2,250
10		$50	$1,000	$1,250	$1,500	$1,750	$2,000	$2,250	$2,500

This makes it much easier to see what combinations of hours and pay reach your goal. Basically, for this range of hours worked, you need a minimum of $25 an hour, and that only gets you to your goal if you work at least 50 hours. On the higher end, $50 an hour is great as long as you get at least 20 hours.

Very useful. So let's walk through all the many, many choices you have for conditional formatting of your data.

Apply

There are five categories of conditional formatting: Highlight Cells Rules, Top/Bottom Rules, Data Bars, Color Scales, and Icon Sets

To apply conditional formatting, select the range of cells you want to apply it to, click on the arrow next to Conditional Formatting in the Styles section of the Home tab, hold your mouse over the category you want to use, and then click on the subcategory you want from the secondary dropdown menu:

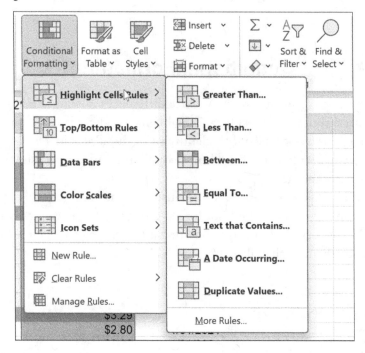

Most options will bring up a dialogue box where you can enter specific criteria and choose a format. Enter the criteria you want to use, choose the format you want, and then click OK. (We'll walk through this in much more detail in a moment.)

Usually I will apply one of the defaults and then go in and edit from there if I want something different in terms of criteria. For example, you may have wondered above why I did over $1199 instead of equal to or greater than $1200. It's because, as you can see in the secondary dropdown menu above, greater than is one of the listed choices, whereas greater than or equal to requires a little more effort to apply.

(In the main dropdown menu, the New Rule option will bring up the New Formatting Rule dialogue box which gives you more choices but also takes more effort.)

Okay, so let's walk through each of the five categories now.

Highlight Cells Rules

You can see the secondary menu for highlight cell rules on the prior page.

Greater Than, Less Than, Between, and Equal To

The first four options there are Greater Than, Less Than, Between, and Equal To. They work pretty much the same. Select the one you want and you'll see a dialogue box. This is the one for Between:

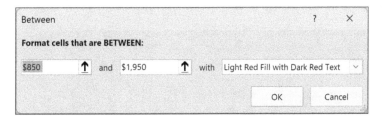

Excel guesses the values you might want to use, but you can just click into each box and type the value you want.

The dropdown on the right-hand side tells you how cells that meet that criteria will be formatted. The default is Light Red Fill with Dark Red Text. The other pre-formatted choices are Yellow Fill with Dark Yellow Text (which I have never used in my life), Green Fill with Dark Green Text, Light Red Fill, Red Text, and Red Border.

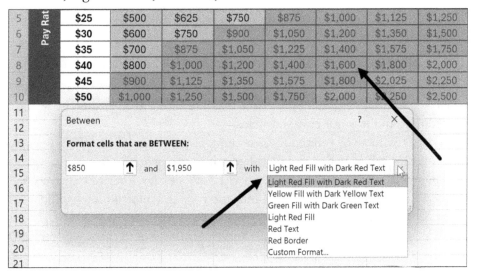

As you can see, whoever put the defaults together assumed you'd mostly want to flag "bad" things since red tends to mean bad in the U.S., especially when used with yellow and green. I personally want to flag things green often, so I almost always have to use that dropdown menu.

If you choose the last item in that dropdown, Custom Format, that will bring up a Format Cells dialogue box where you can apply pretty much any formatting you want to the cells that meet your criteria. If you want purple bolded text with a green striped background, go for it.

(Stripes are under the Pattern Style dropdown on the Fill tab. But just because you can do something does not mean it's actually a good idea to do it. Just sayin'.)

Text That Contains

The highlight cells rules secondary dropdown also has an option for text that contains something. Click on that to get the dialogue box and then type in the text you want. Like so:

1	Royalty Da	Author Na	Marketplace	Transactio	et Units So	Royalty	Currency
2	2021-01-31	Author A	Amazon.com	Standard		1	5.70	USD
3	2021-01-31	Author B	Amazon.com.au	Standard		1	5.03	AUD
4	2021-01-31	Author C	Amazon.com	Free - Price		65	0.00	USD
5	2021-01-31	Author D	Amazon.com	Standard		1	2.76	USD
6	2021-01-31	Author C	Amazon.fr	Free - Price		1	0.00	EUR
7	2021-01-31	Author C	Amazon.ca	Free - Price		3	0.00	CAD
8	2021-01-31	Author A	Amazon.com	Standard		1	5.83	USD
9	2021-01-31	Author C	Amazon.de	Free - Price		3	0.00	EUR
10	2021-01-31	Author A	Amazon.com	Standard		1	1.75	USD
11	2021-01-31	Author A	Amazon.com	Standard		1	2.74	USD
12	2021-01-31	Author A	Amazo					

Text That Contains　　　　　　?　　✕

Format cells that contain the text:

USD｜　　↑　with　Light Red Fill with Dark Red Text ⌄

OK　　Cancel

Note that Excel is applying the conditional formatting in the background even though I haven't yet clicked on OK. Pay attention to this to make sure you're getting the result you want.

I just tested this, and it is not case sensitive.

It will also work with a cell reference, so if the text you want is in a cell in your worksheet, you can click on that cell rather than type the text into the dialogue box.

And it works with wildcard characters. So if I have entries for USD and .com.usd, and I want that second one only, I can type ?usd into the field. Excel will only highlight cells where there is some text in front of usd.

I could also use usd? as my input to only return entries where there is something beyond usd in a cell.

A Date Occurring

Another option in the highlight cells rules secondary dropdown is for a date occurring, but I find this one of limited use because of the choices it gives you:

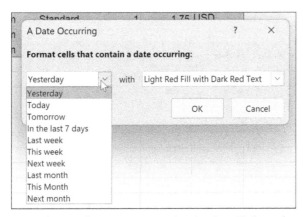

The choices there are yesterday, today, tomorrow, in the last 7 days, last week, this week, next week, last month, this month, and next month. Those are great choices for someone trying to use conditional formatting for something like receivables or payables. You are owed money and you want to see who is past due. Or you need to pay some bills and you want to see which ones are due in the next week so you can pay them.

But I often work with older data sets than that, and as far as I know there's no customizing this one beyond these choices.

Duplicate Values

The final option in that secondary dropdown is for Duplicate Values. I recently used this for a data analysis because I had multiple entries for some case numbers, and I wanted to quickly look at those duplicates to see if they were legitimate, or if someone had double-entered information. This worked well for that because my data was sorted by case number and so the duplicates were right next to each other.

Where it doesn't work as well is when the data is more spread out. Because if you have 10, 10, 20, 20, 30, and 30 at different points in your data, Excel will highlight all six cells the same color even though you technically have three distinct sets of duplicate values.

It also doesn't work as well where there are lots of duplicates.

But for something like subtotals where you want to make sure you didn't have any repeats, it can be pretty useful:

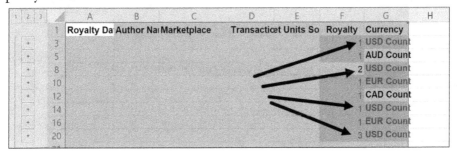

Top/Bottom Rules

Our next category of rules are the top/bottom rules:

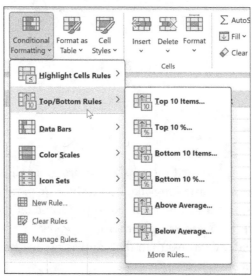

Note that each of the options there in the secondary dropdown uses 10. So top 10, bottom 10, top 10%, bottom 10%. The reality is that when the dialogue box comes up, you can choose whatever number you want to use. Here I changed the value to 3 instead, for example:

(I also changed the color.)

This dropdown also includes a choice for flagging above average and below average results. The average value it will work off is the average you can see in the bottom right corner of your worksheet when your cells are selected.

In this example that is 8, so most of my cells are highlighted as below average because I had a couple of big numbers in the mix:

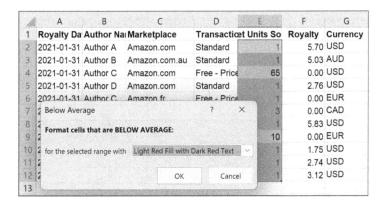

Data Bars

The next category of conditional formats is Data Bars. The secondary dropdown for this one just gives you a choice between solid bars and gradient bars in a variety of colors. By default, he longer the bar the higher the value compared to the other selected cells.

Initially, Excel will determine the range of values to use based on the values in your selected range. Click on More Rules at the bottom of the secondary dropdown menu to set those values yourself via the New Formatting Rule dialogue box:

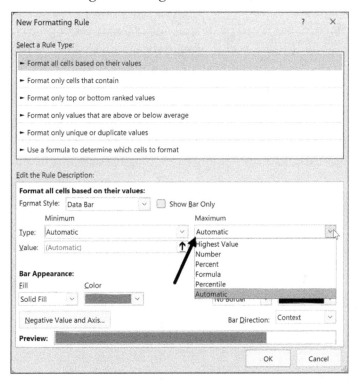

This is also where you can tell Excel to just display the bars and not the associated numbers.

Here are three examples of the green gradient data bar option applied to ten values, but with different settings:

J Default	K Bars Only	L Range of -20 to 20
1		-5
2		-12
3		3
4		4
5		5
6		6
7		7
8		8
9		9
10		10

The first two have values from 1 to 10. The first column is the default data bar setting where the bar gets larger as the number increases, until it fills the cell when the number is the largest in the range. The second is the exact same, except I chose to hide the actual numbers.

With the third one, I made the first two entries negative numbers, and then changed the criteria to say that the range for the data bars was -20 to 20. Since my largest positive value is 10, that cell's bar only covers a fourth of the cell width, half of the positive side. With my negative numbers, the data bar is red by default and, again, doesn't go to the end because the smallest number is -12 but I told Excel the range should go to -20.

Color Scales

Another way to visually see differences across your data is to use color scales. I like to use this one for my monthly revenue, ad cost, and profit numbers. It lets me quickly scan multiple years of monthly values for each, and see if things are going up or down based upon the darkness of each cell.

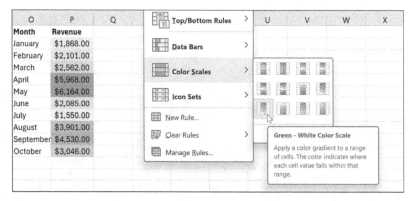

This is another one where you're basically just choosing your color scheme in the secondary dropdown men.

There are a variety of choices that involve green, red, and yellow as well as a couple that involve red, white, and blue instead. I prefer to use a custom color range, because to me red is bad and green is good, so applying a color scheme that uses red and green implies that you've "failed" for the red values and "succeeded" for the green values. But maybe none of them are good. Or maybe all of them are good. So I tend to use different shades of teal or orange or something like that. Like this:

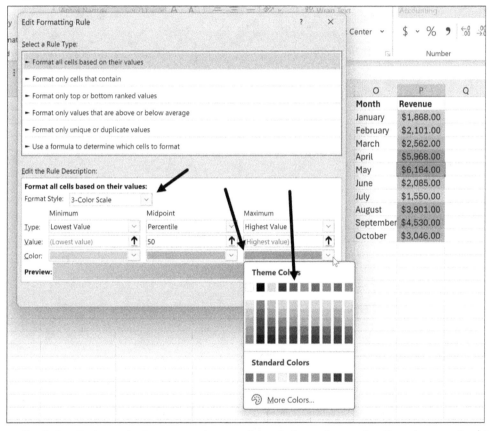

Here I edited the Format Style to use three colors. I then chose the first three colors in that fifth column of the theme colors dropdown menu to create my custom gradient. This blue color is neutral to me in terms of "bad" or "good", but at the same time the difference between the lighter fill color and darker fill color still tells me which months performed the best comparatively.

The default on this one is for Excel to use a percentile to bucket values around the minimum and maximum values in the range, but you can change that. It's possible to set specific numbers instead.

Icon Sets

The final way to visually represent your values is to use icon sets. Icon sets are basically images instead of colors. (Although many of the images also have colors as part of their composition.)

The secondary dropdown menu on this one allows you to choose the images you want to use.

Here I've chosen the "3 Traffic Lights" option that puts a green circle next to the highest values, a yellow one next to those in the middle, and a red one for the lowest values:

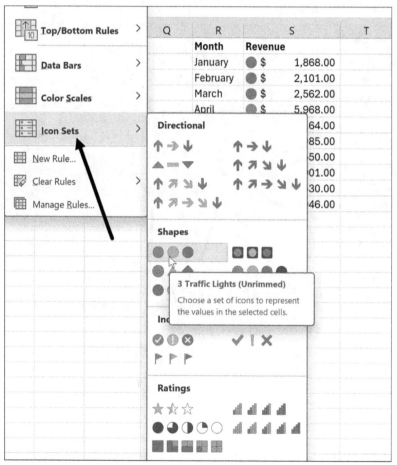

This is another one where if you're going to use it you probably want to customize the ranges used. The default is for Excel to take the values in the range, assign "good" to the top 33%, "okay" to the next 33%, and "bad" to the bottom 33%.

You can also set this one to just show the icons and not the values.

And you can also choose a different icon for each of the three buckets, but I wouldn't recommend it. They're grouped together for a reason.

Manage Conditional Formatting Rules

If you want to edit an existing rule, go to the Conditional Formatting dropdown menu, and choose Manage Rules. That will bring up the Conditional Formatting Rules Manager dialogue box:

At the very top, you can see the dropdown menu for which rules to display. The default is "Current Selection," but you can change that to your current worksheet, any other worksheet in your workbook, or any pivot table in your workbook.

Above, I chose This Worksheet. I also clicked and dragged from the bottom of the dialogue box to make it big enough to show all of the conditional formatting rules I have applied to this worksheet.

Below that dropdown is a row with four main options: New Rule, Edit Rule, Delete Rule, and Duplicate Rule. There is also an up arrow and a down arrow.

And below that is the list of all conditional formatting rules that apply for your selection.

The first column for each rule shows the type of rule (Icon Set, Graded Color Scale, Data Bar, etc).

The next column shows the formatting each rule is using.

The third column shows which cells each rule applies to.

The fourth column has a checkbox for "Stop if True". The checkbox is for situations where you have more than one conditional formatting rule applied to the same cell range. Excel will work through the rules from top to bottom but stop if that box is checked, and the rule was triggered by the contents in the cell.

Edit Rule

To edit a rule that you've already created, click on its row in the rules manager, and then click on Edit Rule at the top of that dialogue box.

That will bring up the Edit Formatting Rule dialogue box. Make the changes you want, click on OK, and you will be brought back to the Rules Manager dialogue box.

If that's all you wanted to do, click OK, the Rules Manager dialogue box will close, and your rule changes will be applied.

If you're not done, you can click Apply to apply that change immediately, or wait until you're done all of your changes and click OK to apply all of them at once.

Above, with the highlight cells rules, if I had wanted to format based on whether the values were greater than or equal to $1200 (instead of greater than $1199), I would have applied one of the default options, and then come here and edited that rule.

As you can see below, the dropdown in the Edit Formatting Rule dialogue box for highlight cell rules, contains greater than or equal to, less than or equal to, and not equal to:

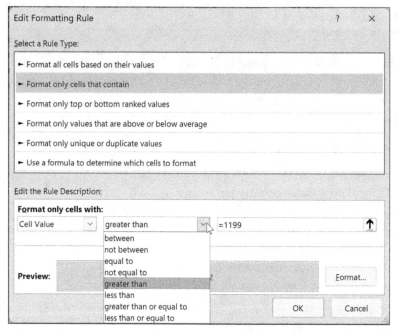

As you can see on the next page, the Edit Formatting Rule dialogue box for the "text that contains" rule will allow you to also format cells not containing, beginning with, or ending with your specified text:

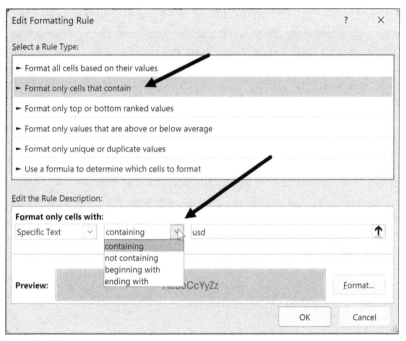

For the top/bottom rules, the Edit Formatting Rule dialogue box also lets you use standard deviations to flag your results:

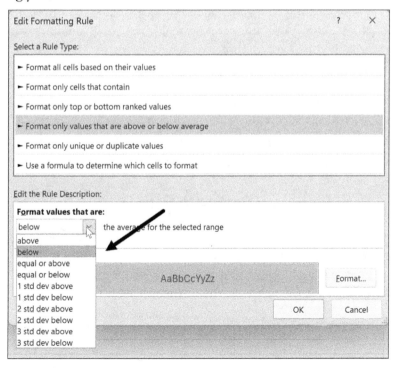

You can also reach the Edit Formatting Rule dialogue box by choosing More Rules at the bottom of any of the secondary dropdown menus, but if you use that option, you may have to change your category to find the correct list of options.

(Also note that you could build these rules from scratch by choosing New Rule from the main conditional formatting dropdown menu at the start, and then choosing the rule type you want, and going from there. I just find it easier to let Excel do most of the work first.)

Clear Rules

To remove conditional formatting, in the main conditional formatting dropdown menu you can hold your mouse over Clear Rules, and then choose to clear rules from the entire worksheet or the selected range of cells.

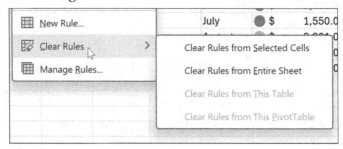

Your other option is to use the Rules Manager dialogue box. If you have a lot of cells that contain conditional formatting, but other conditional formatting you don't want to lose in that worksheet, that's probably the best option.

Delete Rule

To delete a rule, bring up the Conditional Formatting Rules Manager dialogue box by clicking on Manage Rules in the main conditional formatting dropdown menu. Click on the row for the rule you want to delete, and then click on Delete Rule at the top.

Duplicate Rule

To duplicate a rule, bring up the Conditional Formatting Rules Manager dialogue box, click on the row for the rule you want to duplicate, and then click on Duplicate Rule at the top.

Excel will put an exact duplicate of that rule at the top of your rules list. Use Edit Rule to make changes to it. (Or choose Cancel at the bottom to close the dialogue box without saving your changes.)

Multiple Rules On One Cell Range

It is possible to apply multiple conditional formatting rules to the same range of cells. For example, here I've applied red formatting to cells that are under $1,000 and kept the green formatting for cells over $1,199:

	A	B	C	D	E	F	G	H	I
1					Hours Worked				
2			20	25	30	35	40	45	50
3		$15	$300	$375	$450	$525	$600	$675	$750
4		$20	$400	$500	$600	$700	$800	$900	$1,000
5	Pay Rate	$25	$500	$625	$750	$875	$1,000	$1,125	$1,250
6		$30	$600	$750	$900	$1,050	$1,200	$1,350	$1,500
7		$35	$700	$875	$1,050	$1,225	$1,400	$1,575	$1,750
8		$40	$800	$1,000	$1,200	$1,400	$1,600	$1,800	$2,000
9		$45	$900	$1,125	$1,350	$1,575	$1,800	$2,025	$2,250
10		$50	$1,000	$1,250	$1,500	$1,750	$2,000	$2,250	$2,500

If the formatting you apply has no conflict, that's all you have to do. Just select that same range of cells twice and choose your formatting you want for each set of criteria.

But if you have rules that are applied to one cell range where there's a potential for conflict between the rules, then that's where you need to use the up and down arrows in the rules manager and/or the checkbox for Stop if True to make sure that when there's a conflict the correct rule takes precedence.

Conditional Formatting on Pivot Tables

It is possible to apply conditional formatting on a pivot table. To get started, it works the same way. Go to the pivot table, select the cells that you want to apply your formatting to, and apply your conditional formatting. (Be careful not to select subtotal and grand total fields, though.)

By default, Excel is going to set the range of cells covered by your pivot table conditional formatting to just the cells you selected. But for a pivot table, because they are dynamic, you very likely will want that to be set to a different option.

To do that, bring up the Conditional Formatting Rules Manager dialogue box by clicking on Manage Rules in the main conditional formatting dropdown menu.

Select the rule from the list, and choose Edit Rule.

That will give you a set of three options to choose from:

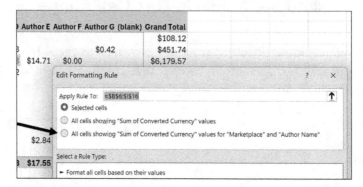

The first is the selected cells. The second is for all cells showing values for that field. The third is for the specific interaction between that field and any others you used to build the values in the table.

In this case that third option is for Sum of Converted Currency for Marketplace and Author Name. That's the one I want. That way if I add a new author or a new marketplace and refresh my pivot table, the conditional formatting will incorporate those changes.

Appendix A: Basic Terminology

Workbook

A workbook is what Excel likes to call an Excel file.

Worksheet

Excel defines a worksheet as the primary document you use in Excel to store and work with your data. A worksheet is organized into Columns and Rows that form Cells. A workbook can contain multiple worksheets.

Columns

Excel uses columns and rows to display information. Columns run across the top of the worksheet and, unless you've done something funky with your settings, are identified using letters of the alphabet.

The first column in a worksheet will always be Column A. And the number of columns in your worksheet will remain the same, regardless of how many columns you delete, add, or move around. Think of columns as location information that is actually separate from the data in the worksheet.

Rows

Rows run down the side of each worksheet and are numbered starting at 1 and up to a very high number. Row numbers are also locational information. The first row will always be numbered 1, the second row will always be numbered 2, and so on and so forth. There will also always be a fixed number of rows in each worksheet regardless of how many rows of data you delete, add, or move around.

Cells

Cells are where the row and column data comes together. Cells are identified using the letter for the column and the number for the row that intersect to form that cell. For example, Cell A1 is the cell that is in the first column and first row of the worksheet.

Click

If I tell you to click on something, that means to use your mouse (or trackpad) to move the cursor on the screen over to a specific location and left-click or right-click on the option. If you left-click, this selects the item. If you right-click, this generally displays a dropdown list of options to choose from. If I don't tell you which to do, left- or right-click, then left-click.

Left-click/Right-click

If you look at your mouse you generally have two flat buttons to press. One is on the left side, one is on the right. If I say left-click that means to press down on the button on the left. If I say right-click that means press down on the button on the right.

Select

If I tell you to "select" cells, that means to highlight them. You can either left-click and drag to select a range of cells or hold down the Ctrl key as you click on individual cells. To select an entire column, click on the letter for the column. To select an entire row, click on the number for the row.

Data

Data is the information you enter into your worksheet.

Data Table

I may also sometimes refer to a data table or table of data. This is just a combination of cells that contain data in them.

Arrow

If I tell you to arrow to somewhere or to arrow right, left, up, or down, this just means use the arrow keys to navigate to a new cell.

Cursor Functions

The cursor is what moves around when you move your mouse or use the trackpad. In Excel the cursor changes its appearance depending on what functions you can perform.

Tab

I am going to talk a lot about Tabs, which are the options you have to choose from at the top of the workspace. The default tab names are File, Home, Insert, Page Layout, Formulas, Data, Review, View, and Help. But there are certain times when additional tabs will appear, for example, when you create a pivot table or a chart.

(This should not be confused with the Tab key which can be used to move across cells.)

Dropdown Menus

A dropdown menu is a listing of available choices that you can see when you right-click in certain places such as the main workspace or on a worksheet name. You will also see them when you click on an arrow next to or below an option in the top menu.

Dialogue Boxes

Dialogue boxes are pop-up boxes that contain additional choices.

Scroll Bars

When you have more information than will show in a screen, dialogue box, or dropdown menu, you will see scroll bars on the right side or bottom that allow you to navigate to see the rest of the information.

Formula Bar

The formula bar is the long white bar at the top of the main workspace directly below the top menu options that lets you see the actual contents of a cell, not just the displayed value.

Cell Notation

Cells are referred to by their column and row position. So Cell A1 is the cell that's the intersection of the first column and first row in the worksheet.

When written in Excel you just use A1, you do not need to include the word cell. A colon (:) can be used to reference a range of cells. A comma (,) can be used to separate cell references.

When in doubt about how to define a cell range, click into a cell, type =, and then go and select the cells you want to reference. Excel will describe your selection in the formula bar using cell notation.

Paste Special Values

Paste Special Values is a way of pasting copied values that keeps the calculation results or the cell values but removes any formulas or formatting.

Task Pane

On occasion Excel will open a task pane, which is different from a dialogue box because it is part of the workspace. These will normally appear on the right-hand side in Excel for tasks such as working with pivot tables or charts or using the built-in Help function. (They often appear on the left-hand side in Word.)

They can be closed by clicking on the X in the top right corner.

About the Author

M.L. Humphrey is a former stockbroker with a degree in Economics from Stanford and an MBA from Wharton who has spent close to twenty years as a regulator and consultant in the financial services industry.

You can reach M.L. at mlhumphreywriter@gmail.com or at mlhumphrey.com.

* * *

If you want to learn more about Microsoft Excel, check out *Excel Tips and Tricks* or one of the main Excel 2024 Essentials titles, *Excel 2024 for Beginners, Intermediate Excel 2024,* or *Excel 2024 Useful Functions.*